By Robyn Freedman Spizman
Published by Ivy Books:

GETTING ORGANIZED
KITCHEN 101
FREE AND FABULOUS
SUPERMARKET SECRETS
MEALS IN MINUTES
QUICK TIPS FOR BUSY PEOPLE

Books published by The Ballantine Publishing Group
are available at quantity discounts on bulk purchases
for premium, educational, fund-raising, and special
sales use. For details, please call 1-800-733-3000.

THE SUPER SHOPPER

QUICK TIPS FOR BUSY PEOPLE

Robyn Freedman Spizman

IVY BOOKS • NEW YORK

An Ivy Book
Published by The Ballantine Publishing Group
Copyright © 1998 by Robyn Freedman Spizman

Cover photo © Philip Shone Photography

http://www.randomhouse.com

Library of Congress Catalog Card Number: 97-94256

ISBN 0-8041-1678-4

Manufactured in the United States of America

First Edition: June 1998

10 9 8 7 6 5 4 3 2 1

This book is dedicated to you, the reader. Whether you're someone who is in a constant hurry or you just need some ways to help you work and play smarter, this book was written especially for you. And to my wonderful parents, Phyllis and Jack Freedman; my family; my friends; my husband, Willy; and our children, Justin and Ali, for all the help, love, and support you give me all year long. You're amazing!

Contents

Acknowledgments   ix
Introduction   1
  1. Quick Tips for Saving Time   3
  2. Quick Tips for Saving Time on the
     Telephone   8
  3. Quick Tips for Saving Money   12
  4. Quick Tips for Kids   20
  5. Quick Tips for Travelers   30
  6. Quick Tips for Gardeners   35
  7. Quick Tips for the Kitchen   38
  8. Quick Tips for Household Cleaning   42
  9. Quick Tips for Movers   46
 10. Quick Tips for the Holidays   51
 11. Quick Tips for Decorating   56
 12. Quick Tips at Work/Office   61
 13. Quick Tips for Weddings   66
 14. Quick Tips for Home Buyers   71
 15 Quick Tips for Entertaining   76
Index   83

Acknowledgments

A quick but heartfelt thank-you to my literary agent, Meredith Bernstein; my outstanding editor, Elisa Wares; Laura Paczosa; and all of the dedicated individuals at The Ballantine Publishing Group. And talk about terrific! My thanks go to the talented Sandy Amann John, who assisted me in all of the research and hard work that was necessary to compile the hundreds of quick tips found in this book. And a special note of appreciation goes to Bettye Storne for her continued support and unending assistance.

Introduction

Always on the run? Do you wish you had an extra hour in every day? Do you find yourself in a race against time? If you answered yes to any or all of these questions, then have I got a book for you! *Quick Tips for Busy People* is the perfect solution for anyone who is on the go and wants to save time, money, and energy.

In this fast-paced lifestyle of ours, saving anything is quite a luxury. But if you hear yourself repeatedly saying, "If I only had more time in the day," then you have arrived at the right place! The timesaving tips in this book are arranged in a variety of categories. No matter who you are or what you do, this book will help you save time and energy doing it.

While the purpose of this book is to make life easier, it's also about working smarter, not harder. If you can do a task in the easiest, simplest manner, then why not? If there's a shortcut that saves you time and still gets the job done, try it. The focus here is to help you make the best use of your time and save you money, too. It'll also guide you toward a more efficient approach to everyday chores and routines.

Quick Tips for Busy People presents a vast

array of simple tips, clever ideas, and handy hints that will earn you time and money in the long run. Use this book as a resource for years to come, and every time you find a tip that works, share it with a friend!

1

Quick Tips for Saving Time

Saving time seems impossible for some of us, but it's possible to gain time by being organized and ready for a task. Managing simple activities and chores is a way of taking charge of your time.

Consider this for a moment: Where or when do you waste time? Do you lose time because you are always looking for things? Do you find yourself doing the same task over and over? Is there never enough time in the day? If any of these questions ring true for you, then you have arrived at the right place.

A bit of organization mixed with an ounce of prevention is the perfect recipe for saving time. So get started and before you know it, time will be on your side, too!

Timesaving Tips

- Place self-sticking notes and a few pens by each telephone and in a few handy drawers throughout the house. You'll save time by not having to search for a pen that works!
- Before you go to bed, make yourself a list of

must-dos for when you wake up. You'll begin your day with a more organized start.

- Keep a grocery list and make it every family member's responsibility to add items. Have a rule: The person who uses the last of anything must add the item to the list.

- Rather than always buying a small or medium container of detergent, shampoo, or whatever, buy the largest size you can. Buy six- or twelve-packs of toilet tissue and paper towels. You'll save time by avoiding repeated trips to the grocery store every time you run out.

- Make it a rule that whenever an item is halfway used up, it must go on the list for your next shopping excursion.

- Plan your day. Break your daily schedule down into things you must do and things that can carry over to the next day. Enter the day with a plan and stick to it if possible.

- Delegate responsibilities and assign chores to family members. Your teenager might be in charge of dry-cleaning runs, while your ten-year-old might make beds or be in charge of taking out the trash. Find an age-appropriate task for everyone.

- Do two things at once. Watch television and give yourself a manicure; talk on the telephone and cook dinner. Find two things that you can easily and safely do at the same time.

- Don't run out to do every errand. Group errands together that are near each other. Before you make a trip, decide if there's a best time to do it.

- Shop during the times that the stores aren't crowded.

- Keep a Rolodex of commonly used telephone

numbers. Keep a stack of blank Rolodex cards near the telephone, and write down a number you need on a card the first time you're given it.

- Begin working on assignments or tasks even if you don't have time to finish them. If you get part of a chore done now, it will take less time later on.
- Prepare two meals at once while you are cooking, or double the portions and freeze half.
- In case you don't have time to cook, be sure to stock up on freezer pleasers—items that make perfect meals in minutes.
- Every time you sew an item, thread up a needle for the next time you need it.
- Wake up fifteen minutes early each day, and jump-start your day.
- Tape a favorite television show and watch it when you have the time. Just think, you can save time while watching the show if you fast-forward the tape through all of the commercials.
- Underschedule one day a week or take the weekend off and give yourself the gift of time.
- Keep on hand duplicates of items you use often, such as scissors and tape. Store them in the rooms where they are most often used.
- Put your purse, keys, or glasses in the exact same place every time and avoid misplacing them.
- Select your clothing the night before. Plan ahead!
- When you find a particular style of stockings or socks that you like, purchase them in quantity.

- Keep an emery board in your car *and* purse.
- Put a clock in every room. Check the time often.
- When you are deciding whether to make a purchase, ask yourself if it's a high-maintenance item that will require too much time to clean. Is it a dust collector?
- Cancel subscriptions for magazines that pile up, ones you really aren't reading.
- Create a filing system for all your papers, and label files so that you know what's in them.
- Scale down your wardrobe to things you really wear and love.
- Choose timesaving gadgets that help you get a job done.
- Save time on cleanup by cleaning as you go.
- When stockpiling things, keep similar items together so that they are easy to find.
- Keep a memo pad in your car for quick notes or messages you need to record.
- Clean your files out often. Reduce paper clutter by keeping only the papers you need.
- Add a colorful sticker to a file you search for and use often. It's easier to identify if you make it look noticeably different.
- Stock up on postage supplies and keep extra stamps on hand.
- Keep a special book for birthdays and check it repeatedly so that you won't miss a special occasion.
- Save business cards in a file box, and if you refer to a card more than once, record it permanently on a blank card and add it to your Rolodex.
- Store your sewing supplies together, but always keep a miniature sewing kit in your

bathroom or in a drawer by your bedside for handy use.

- If you always arrive late, set your watch ahead fifteen minutes.
- Finish as much as possible each day, and start the next one with a clean slate.
- Prepare directions to your home and office and keep copies of them on hand.
- Plan, plan, plan. No matter what you do, you'll save time if you create a schedule for the task. To save time, you must invest time first.

2

Quick Tips for Saving Time on the Telephone

The telephone robs people of lots of time. Talking on the phone can also be a pleasurable experience and a wonderful pastime. However, if you are not doing a terrific job managing telephone calls, then this chapter was meant for you!

The telephone can work for or against you. Do you always feel guilty when you answer and can't talk? Are you plagued by wrong numbers, unsolicited callers, or well-meaning friends and family, and don't know how to say you're way too busy to talk? If so, help has arrived!

Tips to Free You from Being Tied Up or Tied to the Telephone

- Don't pick up the telephone if you are really busy. Learn how to resist the urge. If it's really urgent, most people will call back immediately.
- Own a portable phone so that when you are expecting an important call, you can take it wherever you are.
- Add a call-back service to your telephone

options. If you want to see who called, you can retrieve the number and call the person back if you wish. You can also purchase a gadget that screens your calls and tells you who is calling. Then it's your call whether to pick up!

- Give your children and spouse a code. Just in case you aren't answering the telephone and they need you, instruct them to call and let the telephone ring twice, then hang up and call back. This two-ring signal will let you know it's them.
- Don't play telephone tag. To avoid a lengthy game of trading phone calls, leave a detailed message saying when you'll be available to talk. Consider making a telephone appointment if the call is really important or you keep missing someone.
- Get an answering service or machine that takes your calls and allows you to check for your messages from wherever you are. This service is very helpful because you won't miss a call and you can return the call when you want.

How to Make Your Telephone Calls Short but Sweet

No time to talk? Here are some tips for getting off the line in a flash!

- If you answer the telephone but have no time to talk, when the caller asks if you have a minute, respond, "Forgive me, but I just have a second. Tell me what this call is in reference to and I'll call you back as soon as possible."

- If you're calling someone and have only a minute, tell them, "I have only a minute to speak, but I was wondering if you'd like to join me for lunch tomorrow." Keep it brief and tell them you'll call back as soon as you have time to talk.
- If you have to get off the line abruptly, apologize that you must get off the line, but ask the party when would be a good time for you to call back. If you can't call back, say, "Forgive me, I have a time conflict today, but I'll call you back when I have more time to talk."
- If you receive a call and you have only a few minutes to speak, tell the person on the line that you have only a specific amount of time: "I have only five minutes to talk, but we can talk at another time. Let's go ahead and get started."
- If you receive a lot of unsolicited calls, ask when you receive the call, "Is this call unsolicited?" If the caller says yes, reply, "I'm sorry, we don't accept unsolicited calls."
- If someone calls and says, "Is this Mr. Brown?" ask who's calling before you say yes. Before you give your name out, make sure you know who is on the line.
- If all else fails and you must get off the telephone, try saying in a matter-of-fact voice, "Forgive me, I really must go. I'm sorry, but I'm out of time" (and stick to it!).

Things You Can Do While You're on the Telephone

- File your nails. Keep an emery board nearby.
- Organize your desk.
- Clean out a drawer.
- Use a cordless telephone and begin making dinner.
- Unload your dishwasher.
- Exercise.
- Cut out coupons.
- Make a grocery list or to-do list.
- Spell-check a document on the computer.
- File papers.

3

Quick Tips for Saving Money

Saving money can be quite a challenge. With all of the temptations around us, it's certainly more fun to spend money than to save it. However, in the long run, finding ways to save money does pay off.

To save money, put a strategic plan into place. It's never too late to begin. Ask friends, family members, and people you respect who they consulted about managing their money and what they learned when they did.

The following tips will give you some simple ideas that will add up over time. Keep in mind, though, that these only scratch the surface. There are dozens of ways to become more efficient with money, and you need to get up-to-date yearly with all of the new laws and trends affecting your financial future.

Questions to Ask Yourself

- How much income do I generate monthly? List your monthly income.
- How much do I spend monthly? List your expenses.

- Does my monthly income exceed my expenses?
- What expenses can I reduce? Create a plan to approach this goal.
- What expenses do I anticipate in the near and far future? Add them to the list to begin saving for.
- How much money will I save each week? How much will I save in one month?
- How can I begin saving and managing that money to its fullest potential?
- What areas of my finances do I need help with? Don't give up until you find a solution that works!

Money-Saving Tips

- Talk to a professional, read books, and get up-to-date advice concerning money management. You can never know too much in this area.
- Think up a way to save a dollar (or more) a day. Just think how much money you'll have at the end of the week, month, and year. Place the dollars in an envelope and deposit them at the end of each month.
- When you write a check, do it legibly. Check yourself and make sure you wrote down all the information carefully and recorded the check.
- Investigate all the areas you can deduct on your taxes, and keep records. Save all the receipts for items that might be deductible, and put them away in appropriately labeled envelopes.

- Keep up with your check register daily. Some people like to leave a space between entries for easy balancing. Start a new page each month and break down what you are spending on a regular monthly basis.
- Balance your check register as soon as your statement arrives. Do the same for credit card charges. The longer you wait, the harder it will be to remember what you spent and where you spent it.
- Keep a careful eye on the cash register when items are rung up. Don't be afraid to ask for a clarification and check your receipts.
- Check your bill carefully when eating out. Don't assume anything is correct until you have reviewed it.
- Photocopy all your credit cards and numbers. Keep the copies stored in a file, and find out what you should do if your cards are ever stolen. Be prepared.
- Read labels and examine the content of what you are purchasing. If you know an item is going to shrink, buy a bigger size. When possible, buy clothes that don't require dry cleaning.
- Shop off-season for fabulous buys that you can wear year-round.
- When it comes to your wardrobe, don't overdo it on trends.
- Pay bills on time to save on finance charges.
- Save gas, money, and time by shopping in the yellow pages first. Not only can you locate the best price, but you can call to be sure they have the item in stock before you make the trip.
- Go shopping when you really have time. Save

your receipts and don't purchase anything you can't return.

- Don't go grocery-shopping when you are hungry, and always make out a shopping list.
- Before you purchase an item, ask to test it. You wouldn't buy a car without driving it, so consider this rule when purchasing anything else.
- Wait until an item goes on sale. Ask the salesperson if it will be going on sale. Leave your name and number and ask him or her to call you, or get a number and call repeatedly.
- Try store brands, which are often as good as more expensive name brands.
- Take good care of your electrical items. Save warranties, and read the instructions before using a product. You'll be less likely to misuse it and harm your investment.
- Learn a new skill. Even if you aren't a do-it-yourselfer, there are still some things you can do to save money, from mowing your own yard to giving yourself a manicure. Choose one chore to do yourself and then treat yourself to a professional service for a chore that you prefer to have someone else do.
- Mend your clothes when they rip or tear. They will last longer.
- Grocery-shop only once a week. Plan your meals ahead. You'll decrease your grocery bill if you eat what you have before you buy more.
- Once a week, have a "clean out the pantry or refrigerator" meal. You'll use what you have on hand and save on groceries.
- When you finish monthly payments on something like furniture, a television, or even a

car, continue to pay yourself at least half of the amount. Save or invest this money!

- Keep in mind that you're likely to spend whatever is in your wallet. So watch how much you have on hand.
- Take your change seriously. Whether you fill a piggy bank or save your loose change in a special drawer, it will add up quickly. This idea works especially well if saving bills is difficult for you. You'll be surprised how much the change will add up to.
- Shop for a bank. Ask questions, make comparisons, and see where you will save the most money. Meet the representative at the bank who will oversee your account and check in on a regular basis to keep everything up-to-date.
- Take your children's outgrown clothing or clothes you never wear to a reliable resale shop. Make sure the clothes are clean and in good shape. Clean out your children's and your closets on a regular basis. Your unwanted clothing may represent a lot of money!
- Consolidate errands whenever possible, saving time, money, and energy.
- What expenses can you do without? If you are wasting a great deal of money eating out, try to eat at home more. See how much you can save.
- Use public transportation, car-pool, bike, or walk whenever possible, instead of driving.
- Keep your car well maintained.
- Buy the best quality you can. It will cost more later if you compromise or cut corners.
- Pump your own gas. You'll save quite a bit of money if you do it yourself.

- Clip food coupons. Just think: if you save $10 a month with coupons, that adds up to $120 a year.
- Take your lunch to work. Save the money you would have spent and then invest it wisely.
- Open the windows! Use less air conditioning.
- Keep to the speed limit. You'll save money in gas!
- Review the grocery-store circulars to see what's on sale. Stock up on the sale items.
- Share a magazine subscription with a friend. This is a great way to enjoy a magazine and save money.
- Stay out of stores. You'll save loads of money if you don't tempt yourself.
- When you do shop, make a list of things you really need. Shop in your closet first, and make sure you know what you absolutely have to have.
- Shop secondhand stores for furniture before you purchase new. You'll be surprised at the savings and the great finds.
- Before you purchase something for your home, ask yourself, "Will I still want this item ten years from now?" Your best buys over time will be ones you love forever. While your taste might change, the odds are that if you buy something fabulous, you will keep it longer.
- Measure rooms before purchasing items. You'll save money in the long run if the furniture fits the space.
- Have regular maintenance checks for your home, including your hot water heater, air conditioner, etc. Make sure everything is

working properly as you move from one season into another.

- Before purchasing a car, make sure you know its track record. Talk to mechanics and a variety of people who own the kind of car you are considering before buying one. Make sure it has a record of dependability and safety.
- Before buying a large item like a car or furniture, get a second opinion from an authority you respect.
- Make sure, when you select banks and other service-oriented companies you visit often, that they have a location near your home or office. You'll save gas by limiting the number of trips you make.
- Restyle old clothing that still fits. A new collar or a raised or lowered hemline might be all it takes to add new flair to an outdated outfit. Visit a seamstress or tailor to get a professional opinion.
- Create a wish list. List some things you really want; then prioritize your list and save money toward your goal. Every time you're about to spend money on something frivolous, ask yourself, Which would I rather have? Every saved dollar puts you closer to your goal!
- Before you buy something, consider the maintenance costs as part of the price. Evaluate your decision carefully.
- Get a written estimate before you hire someone. Make sure you know what's included in the quoted price, and ask for an itemized estimate.
- Consider withholding a fraction of the agreed-

on price until a job is done. This gives you leverage to make sure a job is done correctly.

- Choose a reliable dry cleaner and get to know the owner. Discuss any concerns you have about items when you take them to be cleaned, and make sure you inspect your clothing after you pick it up.

- If you've run out of ideas concerning what to get family members or your spouse for holidays, birthdays, or special events, here's a solution: simplify the job and make your money count! Consider grouping a few celebrations together and buy something really special for the entire year.

- Don't make split-second decisions or shop when you don't have time. Think before you spend!

4

Quick Tips for Kids

Children are undoubtedly one of life's greatest pleasures. But balancing work, kids, and home can be hard. Children deserve time and attention, but we often become so absorbed with all of our day-to-day responsibilities and chores that we lose sight of what really matters.

The following tips and suggestions will help you save time, money, and energy as you rush from place to place. They will also help you make daily routines simpler and be a smart consumer. By simplifying chores and housework, you'll make your family life less hurried and stressful.

Quick Cleanup Tips

- Have a place and space designated for your child's belongings. Colorful crates and stackable containers are great for holding toys. Organize your child's clothing and toys so that all items belong someplace specific.
- Add hooks and install rods and shelving that your child can reach. This way he'll be able to put things away from the start and get into the habit of helping.

- If your child won't put toys and belongings away, have a "toy gobbler" that gobbles them up for twenty-four hours. Your child will get the picture quickly when his toys disappear temporarily.
- Define the rules. Don't let your toy closets become catch-alls. Involve your child in cleaning them out on a regular basis, and donate toys that your child no longer plays with to a good cause. Have a rule that you can't take out one toy unless you put away another, to reduce toy mania!
- Less is best. Don't purchase every toy in creation. Follow your child's interests and limit the number of toys you purchase. Rotate toys, putting some away for added value. Watch how they become new again when they reemerge.
- Color-code items like place mats, lunch bags, and book bags. This way if one child always has red things and the other blue, you'll always know who left what behind!

Quick Tips for Kids' Routines

- Instruct your child to follow the "get up and go" rule. Here's how this rule works: The night before, your child must select what he is going to wear the next day. This tip will save everyone time and energy, and your child will be dressed in minutes.
- Everyone will be all smiles if your child's nighttime routines are effortlessly completed. The incentive? Tell your child that her teeth

must be brushed before you'll read her a bed-time story. No exceptions!

- Choose a specific time in the evening to close the kitchen. Children are more likely to finish their dinner and dessert if they know there will be no late-evening snacks.

- Make it a family rule that before coming to breakfast every school-day morning, everyone must be completely dressed, with shoelaces tied and hair brushed, too.

- Allow responsible older children to assist in food preparation if you work and can't be home on time. This will be a big help whenever you're short on time.

- Keep a family calendar in the kitchen and make it everyone's job to note special events and dates to remember. Each family member can use a different color pen to make his or her activities easy to spot. Go over the week with your children to make sure everyone's prepared and knows what's going on that week.

- While your children are still young, let each one pick out an alarm clock. Teach them how to set it, and put them in charge. You'll be pleasantly surprised how much easier it is to get a child up when he or she is in charge. But do set your own alarm clock, just in case!

- Don't leave an area without making sure your children check for items left behind. Get your child into the habit of stopping and making sure he has everything he should before leaving home, school, or any other place. This includes book bags, homework, lunches, jackets, and more!

Quick Tips for Saving Money on Kids

- Create a hand-me-down circle: arrange for a few friends with children of different ages to exchange gently worn clothes. Make sure the clothes are clean, and designate the first day of each month as hand-me-down day. Not only will you save money, but it's lots of fun for everyone involved!
- Before you purchase a new outfit, help your child go through his or her closet to see what doesn't fit. You'll be surprised how many things your child probably hasn't even worn.
- Before you buy it, try it. Never purchase clothing your child hasn't tried on and kept on for at least a few minutes. Make sure it's really comfortable before taking it home.
- Build your child's dress-up wardrobe around one pair of dress shoes. You'll save money if you don't have to purchase a different pair for each outfit.
- When you find a reasonably priced pair of shoes that your child loves, purchase a second pair one size larger.
- If a dress becomes too short, add pants to it. Teach your child to be a creative dresser. Just because something doesn't fit anymore doesn't mean it can't be hemmed, recycled, or used in some new way.
- Make a costume bag with odds and ends like your old ties, costume jewelry, or scarves. Your great pretenders will love dressing up and you'll save money when it's time to transform them into a character for Halloween or a school play.
- Have your child test toys before you buy

them, and insist that he make a wish list. Teach your child how to prioritize what he really wants and narrow down his list. Many toys lose their appeal as soon as they come out of the box, so don't run out and buy everything your child asks for.

- If a restaurant doesn't have a child's menu, order appetizer portions for your child. Some restaurants also serve half portions for children at half the price of the regular item.

- Purchase a copy of *The Smart Shopper's Guide to the Best Buys for Kids* by Sue Robinson (Macmillan Spectrum, 1996). This money-saving guide lists hundreds of ways to find bargains in clothing, furniture, and items manufactured for kids.

Quick Tips for Kids on the Go

- Pack up baby's bag and be ready to go in a flash! Keep one bag fully stocked with diapers, a change of clothing, and all baby's needs just in case you have to run.

- Plan your day around your infant. Consider your child first when planning your time, and you'll increase the time you have for yourself! At some point, most infants have a schedule. So consider which chores and activities you can do while your baby is sleeping, as well as things you can do while she is awake.

- When traveling, carry snacks and juice boxes for your child to enjoy. This will save you time and money when she gets hungry.

- It's a child's job to have fun, so consider how

you can make even ordinary outings enjoyable for your child. For example, at the grocery store encourage your child to go on an alphabet search and name the items he spots that begin with each alphabet letter (apples, butter, candy . . .).

- Make it fun while riding in the car. In my book *Kids On Board* (Fairview Press, 1997), I suggest hundreds of car-time activities for entertaining kids. There are miles of smiles packed in this book, from silly games like counting your teeth with your tongue to learning activities like searching for objects that start with the letters in your child's name.

Quick Safety Tips for Kids

- View your home from a child's-eye perspective. Plan ahead and be preventive. Keep cabinets locked and medicines out of reach. Check for the safety hazards in your home and correct them immediately.
- Purchase unobtrusive safety protectors to cover electrical outlets so a child won't be able to stick anything in them.
- Remove sharp objects and cover sharp corners. Even the corners of a coffee table or cabinet can be harmful to a child, so purchase safety products that will protect your child from these edges. If in doubt, move it out!
- Store tools away from children. Lock tool kits and keep small objects out of a child's reach.
- Check doorstops. Even the rubber tip on a doorstop can be pulled off and swallowed.

Remove doorstops or replace them with ones safe for a child.

- Never leave a young child unattended in a bathtub. Children must be supervised; even older children must be taught how to take a bath safely.
- Be prepared for an emergency! Post the poison control number and your pediatrician's phone number near the telephone.
- Interview and get to know a babysitter before you need one. Hire a sitter to come and sit while you are at home, and observe the sitter's interaction with your child. Always check the sitter's references; never assume anything.
- Teach your children how to answer a telephone correctly, and talk to your children about playing safely. They should never approach a car, talk or go with a stranger, or play without supervision. Have a special password that only you and your children know.
- If your child is on-line on a computer, make absolutely sure she understands that she should never give out personal information such as her address, her telephone number, or the name and location of her school without a parent's permission.
- Attend safety fairs in your area, or call your local children's hospital and request any information they can provide on safety.

Quick Tips About Chores and Kids

- Start teaching children when they are young to help around the house. At first they can pretend to help you sweep or vacuum, and before you know it they can pitch in. Match the chore with the child's age so that it is easy to accomplish and gives him or her a sense of helping the family.

• Whenever possible, involve your children in food preparation. From snapping beans to tearing lettuce, they will love assisting you in the kitchen and will be more inclined to eat what they help prepare.

• Encourage age-appropriate tasks for children. Even little ones can be in charge of hugs.

• Give everyone a turn setting the table. Make it fun, and teach your older children how to fold a decorative napkin.

• Give your children a built-in incentive. For example, whoever goes to the grocery store with you and helps put away the food gets to select something special while you are shopping.

• Put a laundry basket in every family member's closet and make it his or her responsibility to carry it to the washing machine when it's full. The littlest ones may not be able to heft the basket, but they will love helping you sort and fold the laundry.

Quick Snacks for Kids

• Choose a variety of low-salt, healthful cereals and snacks and combine them to make your own trail mix. Package it in small containers for a quick snack.

• Let your child use a Popsicle stick to spread a little peanut butter on a piece of celery. Add raisins, and you have a creative version of ants on a log.

- Cut up an assortment of fruits, from strawberries to cantaloupe, into bite-size pieces and skewer them on a straw. Alternate the fruits for a colorful and healthy snack.
- Make a peanut-butter apple by cleaning and coring an apple and filling the opening with peanut butter.
- Here's a fun idea for finicky eaters. Divide the surface of a piece of bread into four even squares and put a different topping on each square. We call this "circus toast" because it reminds us of a four-ring circus. Use colorful toppings like strawberry jelly, cheese, and grape jelly for a colorful snack.
- Purchase a cookie cutter that is almost as big as a slice of bread, and use it to cut out a creative sandwich shape. Try stamping out heart-shaped grilled cheese sandwiches or star-shaped peanut-butter sandwiches. The more creative the cookie cutter, the better! Consider gingerbread men, handprints—you name it. The cookie cutters are also fun for stamping out frozen pancakes before microwaving or toasting them.
- Our daughter loves it when we pour out letters in pancake batter and serve her a tasty version of her name. It's a fabulous breakfast and doesn't require any more time than cooking the traditional round pancake. Plus, your child is bound to gobble up her entire name and not waste breakfast!
- Conduct a taste test. My friend Lorie does this with her kids and they love it! When in doubt about what to serve for a snack or

even a meal, present an assortment of items and have a taste test. It's a fun way to clean out the pantry or refrigerator and get your kids to try new foods they might otherwise pass on.

5

Quick Tips for Travelers

Whether you travel frequently on your job or get away from home only once a year for a vacation, you probably already know that getting there isn't always half the fun. Let's face it: Packing, getting to the airport on time, and spending hours in a stuffy airplane are all boring and time-consuming. But people who travel a lot know how to make travel easier and more pleasurable. Here are some of their suggestions.

Be a Well-Prepared Tourist

- Reading a good guidebook before you go is the best way to get the most out of your vacation. It will help you pick out the sights you don't want to miss and give you clues as to what isn't worth the price of admission. Most public libraries and bookstores have a good selection of guidebooks on both U.S. and foreign destinations.
- If you're going someplace where they speak a language you don't know, get a phrase book or translation dictionary to help you with the basics of communication.
- When visiting a resort with a season, con-

sider going right before the start of the season or right after it ends. The weather is often just as good as it is during the busy period, but the prices are lower and there are smaller crowds to deal with.

Packing Tips

- If you travel a lot, a suitcase with wheels might be one of the best investments you can make. It will really speed you up as you move through the airport. A good piece of luggage will last a long time, so research your choices and make a match for the long haul.
- Items wrinkle when they move a lot and are under constant pressure from other objects. Reduce the movement your clothes will make by shifting constantly, and place plastic dry-cleaning bags between them for fewer wrinkles.
- Bring smaller samples of items like night cream, shampoo, or anything else that is liquid. Pack them in plastic sealable bags or a waterproof pouch in case they leak, and make sure they are positioned away from your clothing.
- Don't forget to pack your child's favorite stuffed toy or a blanket she won't go to sleep without. Think ahead and plan accordingly, especially when you are traveling with children.
- In a carry-on bag, pack your datebook, jewelry, medicine, makeup, or any items you'd really regret losing or simply not having if they were lost in a suitcase you checked, in case your luggage is lost or delayed.

- Limiting yourself to carry-on luggage eliminates the wait for baggage upon arrival and ensures that your suitcase will arrive at the same time you do. But packing a carry-on bag requires some tricks of the trade, including:

Carry only travel-size toiletries and appliances (such as hair dryers).

Have a travel wardrobe that is color coordinated so all the tops work with all the bottoms. Go for lightweight multifunctional fabrics, such as wool gabardine, silk, and cashmere.

Limit the number of shoes you bring.

Take advantage of laundry services at your hotel or hand-wash items as needed.

If you're traveling with a companion, see if you can share a supply of toiletries and appliances.

Tips for Overseas Travel

- If you're renting a car, check with your insurance company before you leave the country. There's a good chance that your policy doesn't cover you when you're out of the United States, and you will have to buy coverage from the rental agency or take your chances on going uninsured (if that's permissible in the country you're visiting).
- Photocopy the key pages of your passport before you go overseas and carry them separately. If your passport is stolen, the copies may help you get a replacement.
- Before you leave home, write down the phone number of the U.S. consulate at your destination, and carry it in a safe place. You'll need that number in case of an emergency.
- Exchange only the amount of money you will

need for a day or two at a time. This will keep you from overspending and will also prevent you from being stuck with lots of foreign currency that you have to exchange back into dollars. (You lose money every time you go through the exchange process.)

- For accurate information about tipping customs, which vary widely throughout the world, ask a local you trust after you arrive.
- Carry all prescription medications in the packaging you got from the pharmacy.

Thoughts from Frequent Flyers

- Keep hand lotion, nasal spray, and other products in your carry-on bag to combat the dry air in the plane's cabin.
- Wear comfortable shoes on the plane.
- Get to the airport about thirty minutes earlier than you think you need to. With increased security measures and other delays, the time will disappear quickly.
- Bring snack foods with you when you travel. Airplane food isn't very filling, and food at airports is often expensive. Snacks are especially handy if your flight is delayed or you land someplace too late to purchase a proper meal.

Keep Safety in Mind

- Put a name and address on your luggage, but use your business address. That way, if your bags are stolen, the thief won't be able to find and rob your house, too, while you're gone.

- Keep your bags close to you at all times in the airport. Don't allow yourself to get distracted and lose track of them. Wrap the luggage strap around your ankle or wrist; otherwise it's an easy target for thieves.
- When staying in a hotel, double-check everyone who knocks on your door. If the person knocking identifies himself as a hotel employee, call the desk and make sure the hotel actually sent someone up and you approve.

6

Quick Tips for Gardeners

There's nothing more inviting than a colorful garden in the spring or summer. True, gardens can require a lot of maintenance, but they don't have to. Gardens can be as spectacular or as laid-back as you want. When you add plants to your garden, do a little research to make sure the ones you select grow well in your climate and in the particular conditions found in your garden. By doing that, you've taken a giant step toward keeping your garden a place of relaxation rather than worry.

Quick Buying Tips

- Perennial flowering plants are the gardener's best friend. While they are initially more expensive than annuals, they will bloom year after year, saving you the time and expense of putting in new plants each spring. Additionally, many perennials reproduce, giving you even more bang for your gardening buck, so don't be put off by the higher price tag.
- Annual flowering plants are useful for a quick splash of color or in a spot that perennials will eventually fill in.

35

- Buy plants with at least one bloom so that you can be sure what color the flower will be.
- The most interesting gardens contain a mix of plants of varying heights, colors, foliage styles, and blooming periods. If you don't feel comfortable selecting such a mix yourself, study catalogs from garden supply houses. Many employ designers who create the gardens pictured in the catalog. When you find a design you like, consult the list of plants in that garden and select some to use in your own, feeling assured they will partner well.

Work with Mother Nature, Not Against Her!

- Be generous with mulch. It will help keep moisture in the ground, so you'll have to water less, and it will help to discourage the dreaded weeds.
- Use rubbing alcohol to disinfect the shears between cuts when you're pruning a plant you think has a bacterial infection.
- Instead of spraying your tomato plants to kill bugs, let nature help you out. Plant marigolds, poppies, or nasturtiums near your tomatoes. The flowering plants will attract insects that eat aphids and other pests that attack tomatoes. And you get a flower garden spot, too!
- To water a garden plant with deep roots, take a good-size coffee or other such can, remove the bottom of it with a can opener, and then dig a hole for the can next to the plant, where it can be permanently placed. Pour water directly into the can, and water will go straight to the plant's roots.

Quick Tips for Getting the Most out of Bulbs

- If you are worried about squirrels and other animals digging up newly planted bulbs, cover the area with screening. Be sure to remove it before the plants come up in the spring.
- Many bulbs do best when their foliage is allowed to die back naturally, so cut off the old blooms when they wither, but don't cut back the leaves. If the foliage looks scraggly, put a rubber band around the leaves or take one leaf and wrap it around the others to pull them together and make them more presentable.
- If you'd like to keep your tulips in the ground rather than digging up the bulbs each year and replanting them in the fall, plant the bulbs two to three inches deeper than recommended.
- When flowers from bulbs, such as tulips or daffodils, become overcrowded, dig them up, divide them, and replant the little bulbs. The smallest ones might not grow, but there's no harm in trying.

7

Quick Tips for the Kitchen

Does dinnertime sneak up on you without warning? Is meal preparation your most dreaded, time-consuming task? Funny, isn't it—our kitchens are packed with timesaving appliances, but we still don't seem to have enough time to cook.

You can do plenty of things to make your time in the kitchen more productive. I make it my mission to find quick and easy recipes my family will eat, for one, and I use leftovers whenever I can to build another day's dinner.

Here are some other things you can do to work smarter and faster in your kitchen.

Preparation Is the Key

- Always read the recipe before you begin cooking. Make sure that you have all the ingredients on hand and that you know in what order items are mixed together. (Pencil brackets around groups of ingredients, if that helps you.)
- For most recipes, it makes sense to have everything cut up, chopped, measured, and ready to go before you start cooking. This is especially important in stir-fry dishes and

other meals where the actual cooking time is short.

- Learn to measure common ingredients, such as salt, by approximation. Try pouring a teaspoon of salt in your hand and see what it looks like. Now you can guesstimate. Don't use this method for baking, where precisely measured ingredients make all the difference.
- Use cooking spray to make cleanup easier. Spray it on graters, food processor blades, and beaters of a mixer before you use the utensil.

Quick Tips About Spices

- Many people store their spices above the stove, because it's convenient when they are cooking. But heat will destroy the flavor of spices, which should be stored in a cool spot. Red spices, like chili powder, keep their flavor best when they are refrigerated.
- In most recipes, you can substitute a teaspoon of dried herbs for a tablespoon of fresh, chopped herbs, or vice versa.
- Arrange your spices in alphabetical order on your spice rack or shelf. You can see what you have—and find what you need—much faster that way.

Freezer Tricks

- Freeze leftovers in serving-size freezerproof microwavable containers: individual meals in an instant.
- Buy family-size packs of meat, but when

you get them home, rewrap the contents in smaller packages for freezing so you will have appropriate amounts for cooking.

- Save leftover cooked vegetables together in a container in the freezer. When the container is full, make some chicken broth, add the veggies, and you have homemade vegetable soup.
- You can also freeze leftover bits of meat and use them in a potpie or casserole.

Tips for Grocery Shopping

- Bigger is not always cheaper. So-called economy packs are sometimes more expensive than smaller packages.
- Carry a small calculator with you so you can determine which is the best buy based on cost per unit (such as ounce).
- Always shop with a grocery list, and religiously write down everything you need before you leave home. (Get in the habit of writing the item down when you notice it's almost gone, then check the refrigerator and pantry for items you are running low on before going shopping.) There is nothing more irritating or time-consuming than returning to the store because you didn't buy something you really needed.
- Learn the layout of the stores you frequent. Knowing which products are shelved where will save you time when you run into the store to grab one or two specific items, and it will help you avoid walking down an aisle where there's nothing you buy. It will also

allow you to steer your kids away from any aisle you consider too tempting for them.

- Buying store brands can often save you money. No matter how happy you are with expensive name-brand items, make a habit of trying at least one store-brand product each time you shop. Pick one that's on sale, if that will make you feel better. You might not like every generic item, but if you can switch to even a few of the lower-priced goods, you'll save a lot over the long run.

- At the grocery store, you often face a choice: your time or your money. Prepared or convenience foods cost a lot more than unprocessed ingredients. Some prepared items might be worth the price, but some aren't. For example, do you save enough time buying premixed orange juice to justify a price double that of orange juice concentrate?

Quick Tips for Household Cleaning

Let's face it. Housework isn't really hard, but it does take time, minutes of the day or weekend that you could put to good use doing something you enjoy more. To me, anything that makes housework quicker and easier is good news! Here are some ways I've found to speed up household chores.

General Cleaning Tips

- Use cleaning products for multiple purposes. Window cleaner, for example, can be used on almost all the surfaces in your kitchen and bathroom, including ceramic tile, stainless steel, chrome, appliances, and glass. By using just one product you'll save money because you aren't buying lots of different kinds of cleaners.
- Assemble all the supplies you'll need for cleaning and keep them together in a bucket or other container you can carry from room to room. Keep the bucket stocked with a spray bottle of cleaning solution, paper towels, a scrub brush, a dust rag, and aerosol wax. When it's time to clean, just grab the

bucket and go. This will save you time chasing after everything you need each time you're ready to clean.

- When dusting, remember more dust settles on horizontal surfaces than on vertical ones. In other words, you have to dust the top and bottom of a picture frame (or bureau or whatever) more often than you have to dust the sides.
- Dust first, then vacuum. Otherwise, you're knocking dirt to the floor after you've already cleaned it.
- Put mats at all the outside entrances to your home so family and visitors can wipe mud and dirt off their shoes before entering the house. Once you have your family trained, you will definitely notice the difference.
- Check the furnace and replace the air filters on air conditioners regularly to cut the dust in your home.

A Quick Cleaning Tip

An old toothbrush makes a handy cleaning tool. Some things it's useful for:

Scrubbing stains on laundry
Cleaning the grout between the tiles on the countertop or shower
Cleaning behind the faucet and other hard-to-reach areas

Quick Tips for Laundry

- If the care label on a garment says Dry Clean rather than Dry Clean Only, you might be able to wash it instead of paying to have it dry cleaned. Test the fabric for colorfastness before ruling out dry cleaning.

- To test fabric for colorfastness, place a part of it that won't be noticed—such as the edge of an inside seam—on a paper towel. Take a wet cotton swab and press it firmly on the fabric. If no color bleeds onto the paper towel, it is probably safe to wash the item.

- Many silk items are washable, but do not put them in your dryer. The heat can cause the silk to disintegrate. Roll the wet garment in a towel to absorb moisture, then hang it to dry.

- Treat all stains as soon as possible, because fresh stains are much easier to remove than stains that have already set.

- Hot water can set some stains, so always start treatment with cold water.

- When treating a stain, place it facedown and treat the back of the stain, so you don't force the stain deeper into the fabric.

- Pretreat small stains with undiluted liquid detergent or a paste of powdered detergent and water. When stains cover a large area or are not fresh, presoak the garment in water with color-safe bleach or powdered detergent.

- Powdered detergents usually remove dirt and clay better than liquids and are cheaper. Liquid detergents are better on many greasy, oily food stains.

- Don't put a fabric softener sheet into the dryer after the drying cycle has started. The fabric softener can leave spots on clothes if it is heated up too quickly.

Quick Tips on Cleaning Appliances

- If thoroughly washing the inside of your refrigerator does not eliminate an odor, try this: Pack the refrigerator with crumpled sheets of black-and-white newspaper. Place charcoal briquettes randomly throughout the newspapers. Close the doors and let stand for at least 24 hours. Remove briquettes and papers and wash all interior surfaces again.
- A paste of baking soda and water makes a mildly abrasive cleaner that can be used on surfaces of appliances, such as baked enamel or porcelain enamel, that would be scratched by a harsher abrasive.
- To make cleaning the porcelain cavity of an oven easier, put a half cup of household ammonia in a shallow glass container and leave it in the cold oven overnight. The fumes from the ammonia will help loosen burned-on grease and food.
- To remove any odor in your dishwasher, fill the detergent cups with baking soda. Start the regular wash cycle and let it run for about 10 minutes, then stop it. Let the dishwasher sit overnight, then complete the wash cycle.

9

Quick Tips for Movers

Any move, whether it's across the street, across town, or to another state, can be hectic and unsettling. Things can get lost, broken, or forgotten, and members of your family may feel overwhelmed by the experience. But organization and planning can make moving day— and the days before and after the van pulls up to your door—go more smoothly. Here are some tips to make your moving experience a good one!

Quick Tips on Getting Ready

• As soon as you find out you might be moving, go through your family's belongings and pick out items you no longer want or need. Hold a garage sale to get rid of all that stuff. You'll probably make enough to pay for the move. And there will be a lot less to pack and unpack.
• Get estimates from three movers. Compare what each company offers and get recent references. Be sure to read and understand the contract before signing up with any moving company.
• Try to move on a weekday. Movers often

charge less and are easier to book during the week than on weekends. There will be less neighborhood traffic to deal with, too, if you move on a weekday.

Quick Tips for Address Changes

- Make a list of everyone you must notify of your address change. (Monitor your mail for a month before the move to get a good idea of who needs to know about your new address.) Check each party off the list as you notify them. To get you started, here are places you might need to notify of an address change. Add others as you see fit.

Banks
Mutual fund companies
Stockbrokers
Credit card companies
Insurance agents/companies, including health, life, auto, boat, home-
      owners, or renters
Church or synagogue
Alumni association
Professional organizations
Any club you or a member of your family belongs to
Magazines and other periodicals you subscribe to
Doctor, dentist, pediatrician, and other health care providers
Book and record clubs
Lenders for any loans you are paying off
Health club
Post office

- Use toll-free customer service numbers to change the addresses on as many accounts as possible. That's much faster than sending letters.

- To let friends and family know of your new address, design a postcard with the pertinent information. For example, you can use a graphic of a cow and say, "We're moo-ving," or an outline of the state you're headed for and say, "The Browns are Texas bound!" Have duplicates made at a copy shop and send the cards to everyone on your holiday card list.

Quick Tips for Packing

- Number your boxes consecutively and keep a master list detailing the contents of each. As the movers bring the boxes into your new home, check each one off the master list. This way, you can be sure all the boxes have arrived.
- Label each box with the number that corresponds to the master list. Also label it with the room it should be placed in when it arrives at the new house. As you stand at the door checking off the boxes, you can direct the movers where to deposit each one.
- Limit the contents of any box to items that will be used in one room. That way, you won't have to carry things from room to room as you pack and unpack.
- Before the moving truck leaves your new home, inspect the van to make sure that nothing has accidentally been left in the truck; lamps, sofa cushions, and other small,

unboxed items are the things most likely to be overlooked.

- Clearly mark boxes that must be opened immediately. This will help you know what to do first. Usually it's best to unpack the boxes with your kitchen supplies first and then those with stuff from bathrooms and bedrooms, since they are the ones that hold items used daily.

- Pack up your child's favorite belongings in a special box and let him unpack it. This helps your child feel more comfortable in his new surroundings and gives him a role in the move. If children unpack their special items first, they are usually more cooperative and content. Besides which, they'll have something to play with!

- Have drinks and snacks on hand. Think of ways to keep everyone happy and make the experience as positive as possible.

- Allow willing friends to really help. You'll be surprised at how many extra hands you can use when moving. Don't act like a martyr! Let others assist you. The day of the move, you'll be glad you did.

Quick Tips for Long-Distance Movers

- Instead of paying a deposit with utilities in your new town, see if they will accept a letter from your old utility company stating that you have kept your account up in a timely manner. Then don't forget to ask your old utility company to send such a letter.

- For a month or two before you move, subscribe

to the local newspaper of the town you are moving to. When you relocate, you'll feel less like a stranger because you'll already know something about the community and will be familiar with local names, organizations, and issues that make the news. Peruse the newspaper ads to get an idea of where the best deals are, and you will already know where to shop by the time you move.

- Contact local branches of clubs and support groups you already belong to in your new city before you move. They will be glad to welcome you and share helpful tips about your new location.
- Consider renting rather than buying a home at first, especially if you are moving to an area you are totally unfamiliar with. I'm sure you don't want to move twice, but if you rent for a while, you will have a much better handle on such matters as where the good school districts are or what areas are best for commuters. Buy in haste, and you may end up moving twice anyway.

10

Quick Tips for the Holidays

There's nothing like a holiday to raise the stress level of a busy person. You've already got plenty to do, and now you're being bombarded by magazine articles on the perfect holiday dinner or the perfect holiday decorations or the perfect holiday outfit. I've got plenty of tips on a variety of holidays, but this is the most important thing to remember: Enjoy your holidays!

Quick Tips Through the Year

• One way to make your holidays less hectic is to move the emphasis away from food and gift-giving back to the original intent of the holiday. Whether it's Easter, Thanksgiving, Passover, Christmas, or Kwanza, get your family to focus on the deeper meaning behind the event. Gather together and read relevant sacred passages, discuss things you are thankful for, or volunteer to do something for a needy family. It might end up being the most memorable holiday your family has ever had.

• Shop clearance sales after the holiday. No, the candy won't last for twelve months, but holiday-themed partyware, decorations, wrapping paper, or even clothing can all be purchased at a deep discount and stored until the next year. Just note on your calendar where you stashed it so you won't waste time looking for things.

New Year's Eve

- A New Year's Day brunch is cheaper and easier to organize than a New Year's Eve party. And you'll find your friends are available that day and eager for a relaxing get-together.
- Stay home with the kids and have a party with one or more other families. Rent tapes, plan a few games, and let everyone be a part of the arrangements. Your guests can bring a few dinner items already prepared and ready to serve.
- For a quick cleanup, purchase sturdy, colorful paper plates and have a few trash bags on hand. Stick to paper for a no-mess meal that night.

Independence Day

- Have any friends who work in tall buildings? Their office window might provide a great spot from which to view the fireworks, if they can get access on a holiday.
- Let everyone contribute something for a potluck July Fourth lunch or dinner. Give them one assignment, however: their food presentation must include something that is

red, white, and blue. This requirement will ensure that your buffet will look fabulous, from creative platters and decorative touches to strawberry-covered salads, and all will enjoy viewing everyone else's creativity.

Halloween

- If you're in a hurry or just reluctant to wield a knife, use a permanent black marker or non-toxic paint to paint a face on a pumpkin, rather than carving it. It won't glow in the dark, but it looks fine in a lighted area.
- Shop consignment stores for used costumes for your kids. Secondhand stores can also be a great source of items that can be used to create costumes from scratch.
- Wearing all black for a witch or all orange for a cat makes an inexpensive and quick costume base. Add a witch's hat or kitten's ears for the finishing touch.

Thanksgiving

- Chances are you know exactly what you'll fix for Thanksgiving dinner months in advance. Keep that in mind, and as the staples you'll need go on sale, stock up and store them in the freezer or pantry until needed.
- Prepare your recipes in stages. Early in the week, measure and mix all the dry ingredients and put them aside until Thanksgiving Day, when you can add the moist ingredients and cook the food.

- Prepare ingredients you will need in several dishes, such as chopped onions, in bulk in your food processor before you actually start assembling the dishes.
- For safety's sake, *don't* prestuff your turkey.

Christmas and Hanukkah

- To save time stringing lights on the tree each year, buy an artificial tree that is stored in sections. String lights on each section individually, and they can remain that way as long as you own the tree.
- If you never include a letter with your holiday cards, why not send postcards? There's no need to seal envelopes, so it's faster. Postage is cheaper, too, if you buy postcard stamps.
- Put a metal tray or aluminum foil under the menorah before lighting the candles. This will make for easier cleanup and save your counter from excess candle drippings.

Shopping for Gifts

- Take a generic calendar that doesn't list the specific days of the week and record everyone's birthday and special dates on it. Refer to it yearly.
- Spread your holiday shopping throughout the year. Buy gifts at craft fairs, in unusual shops you come across when traveling, and during sales. You'll be giving more interesting gifts, and you'll avoid the stress of

December shopping—and the bite of January credit card bills.

- Carry a list of people you need to buy gifts for in your wallet. Include clothing sizes and other information that would be helpful if you decide to buy a gift on the spur of the moment.

11

Quick Tips for Decorating

Do you love to look at magazines full of photos of attractively decorated rooms, but resist the temptation to do anything with your own home? That's the situation with many people, who fear making costly mistakes they will have to live with for years to come. But decorating your home doesn't have to be expensive or time-consuming. By using a few of my tips, such as quick and easy ways to add color to your home, you can have a whole new look in just a short time. You can change it with the seasons. Here are some helpful ideas to get you started.

Quick Tips for Being a Smart Shopper

- Anytime you see a photograph of a room you particularly like, tear it out of the magazine and put it in an idea file. When you are ready to redecorate, refer to the file and see what ideas you can use from the rooms you admired.
- One of the quickest, cheapest, and easiest ways to change the look of a room is to paint the walls a different color.
- Before painting a room, bring home color

cards from the paint store to see what the color looks like in the room you want to paint. The lighting in any room will make the color look different on the walls. If you can't tell from the color card, buy a small can of the paint and apply it to a small section of one wall to see how it looks.

- Buy the best quality you can at a given time and prioritize your purchases. It's better to buy one really good item than lots of mediocre ones. Over time they will be your best investments in decorating.

- Limit the use of trendy fabrics and things you'll outgrow quickly over time. Stick to quality furniture or art you really value and will still love five years from now. If you're set on using what's in right now, do so with pillows or chairs that can easily be re-covered.

- Always buy enough paint at one time to cover all the wall space. Even with computerized color mixing, there can be slight variations in color if the paints aren't mixed at the same time.

- When purchasing wallpaper, be sure to buy enough at one time and make sure all the rolls are from the same dye lot. Rolls from different lots can have slight but noticeable differences in coloration.

- Keep the large, expensive elements of your decorating scheme—carpeting, large upholstered furniture, and custom draperies, as well as tile and plumbing fixtures in a bathroom— neutral in color. (At the very least, avoid making them trendy shades you might tire of quickly.) Introduce a livelier accent hue through accessories.

58   Robyn Freedman Spizman

- Try it before you buy it. Before making a purchase permanently yours, ask the clerk if you can try the item on a trial basis. Sometimes there will be a restocking or pickup fee, while other times you can actually have it delivered and try it at no cost. This will save you from an expensive mistake, and it is worth the small fee you might have to pay to send it back if it isn't right.

Cheap and Easy Ways to Add Color

If you want to change the color scheme in a room or add an accent color, do it in a way that will be easy to modify when you pine for a different shade later on. Here are some quick, easy, and relatively inexpensive ways to put a splash of color in a room:

Accent pillows
Area rugs
Candles
Wall hangings
Planters
Wallpaper borders
Accessories such as baskets, vases, and knickknacks
Towels in the kitchen or bathroom
Shower curtain in the bathroom
Slipcover on a chair or sofa

Questions to Ask a Decorator

Sometimes it's smart to get professional advice before redecorating a room. When you interview an interior decorator, get the answers to these questions:

- How is the decorator paid? Does she charge an hourly rate or earn a commission off the items she sells you?
- Does he have experience working with the kind of budget you have in mind? Is he comfortable with that range?
- Can she provide you with the names and telephone numbers of former clients who will serve as references?
- If you simply want guidance on issues such as rearranging your furniture or suggestions on how to accessorize a room, would the decorator be willing to act as a consultant at an hourly rate?
- Is the decorator comfortable listening to and incorporating your ideas?
- What can you do to prevent costly errors? What if you don't like the decorator's choices?

Discuss the what-ifs ahead of time, and make sure you understand clearly what you are ordering or doing.

Good Decorating Reflects Your Needs

When thinking about redoing a room, it's easy to focus all your attention on the color scheme, but there are some other things to consider:

- Pick a decorating style that suits your lifestyle, which could be casual or formal.

- If you have kids and pets, select fabrics, furniture, and wall coverings that will stand up to wear and tear.
- If you plan to eat in that room, choose fabrics that will survive the snacks and late-night dinners.
- Remember that lighting is an important element in any design. You'll need different sources of light to set the tone of the room, to highlight artwork or other elements of interest, and to provide illumination in areas where you will perform specific tasks, such as reading or doing crafts.
- When planning a space, think about telephone outlets and where wires will run. Where will the telephone sit? If you have company over, what will you serve food on? Where will you store other items you use daily?
- If limited space is a problem, make rooms multifunctional. For example, a sleeper sofa is an obvious solution if you don't have a guest room. Maybe your sewing machine could take up a corner in the dining room. When you have guests over, cover the sewing machine with a tablecloth and use it as a sideboard.
- Chairs are more versatile than large sofas. Before you make a major purchase, consider how you might use that item later on if you change the room around or redecorate. Think ahead!

12

Quick Tips at Work/Office

Working smarter isn't just a slogan—it's a survival technique. Efficiency and productivity are the keys to keeping your job in this day of the lean, mean corporation. For people whose jobs revolve around papers, meetings, and phone calls, being more productive often means making simple changes in the way you work. Being organized, being clear on what's a priority, and taming the meeting monster are some simple steps you can take to increase your efficiency. (If it's the telephone that slows you down, turn right now to chapter 2 and get the phone under control.)

Quick Tips for Setting Priorities

- Take a few minutes at the start of each day to list what you need to get done during that day and the rest of the week. Try to prioritize the tasks. During the day, cross off those that get done and add new chores as they come up.
- If you deal regularly with deadlines, especially other people's deadlines, find out ahead of time exactly what they are. You'll be

surprised how much this will help. Sometimes you have more time than you ever imagined, and other times you'll need to work overtime to meet the deadline. Get the facts!

- Don't let anyone set your priorities for you. Just because an item comes by overnight delivery or with a fax cover sheet headlined Extremely Urgent, it isn't necessarily any more important than what you are already working on. Take a look at it and decide where it fits on *your* priority list.

Get Off the Meeting Treadmill

If meetings seem to consume most of your day and prevent you from doing your work, take action:

- Set an example by keeping any meeting you are in charge of short and focused. Distribute an agenda before the meeting, and stick to it.
- If you're invited to a meeting to provide specific information, see if your input can be in written form or delivered verbally to someone before the meeting so you don't have to attend.
- Assess your behavior in meetings. If you're contributing to long, unproductive meetings because you are unprepared or because you spend a lot of time chatting about unrelated issues, clean up your act. Others may follow your lead.
- Make sure you get as much information as

you can during the meeting in order to be able to do your job when you leave.

Let Technology Help You

- Learn to make the most of your computer and its software. If you don't feel you understand the software well enough to use it to its maximum efficiency, see if your human resources department (or whoever handles training at your company) offers classes. If none are available through your company, consider taking one at a private computer training center; the increase in efficiency will be well worth the fee for a class. At the very least, spend a couple of hours studying the manual and learning as much as you can on your own.
- If you have a job where you call several phone numbers repeatedly, request a programmable phone. Once you've programmed in the numbers, you'll never have to look them up again.
- Explore your high-tech options, those things technology can do to help you save time. For instance, check out fax machines that allow you to program in multiple numbers when sending the same fax to many locations. You'll be surprised at how much time and energy you can save every day by working smarter.

Quick Tips to Help You Organize Yourself at Work

- Straighten up your desk and put things where you can find them. Start a file folder for each project you are working on, and set them by your computer or telephone, where you can reach for one as needed. If you work on several projects at a time, take a five-minute break two or three times a day if necessary, and refile all the papers scattered around your desk. This will pay off in better efficiency and less time spent looking for a key piece of paper.

- Have trouble keeping track of when projects are due? Get a calendar—a big one—and tack it to the wall beside your desk, where you can refer to it regularly. Every time you are assigned a new project, make a habit of putting any deadlines related to it on the calendar. Make a ceremony of crossing projects (or steps completed) off the calendar as they are finished.

- Clean out your desk drawers and start fresh. Return all those unused pens, paper clips, and other items to the supply cabinet. Get a few of everything you need (two black pens, two red pens, a couple of legal pads, sticky notes, etc.), resisting the temptation to stock up on everything or take items you never use. Then use a drawer organizer so you can find what you need when you need it. (A kitchen drawer organizer will work fine.)

Quick Travel Tips to and from Work

- If you have the option, take public transportation or join a car pool rather than driving to work each day. You'll be amazed at how much stress you avoid by not driving through rush-hour traffic, and you can put the time spent on the train or bus to good use.
- Use travel time on the bus or train to read reports or professional journals; write, edit, or proofread work-related documents; plan presentations; or put together the day's to-do list and set priorities. You can also take advantage of the quiet time for some quality thinking and creativity.
- Install a car telephone to make sure that if you're running late and need to make an important call, a telephone is at your fingertips. Have all of your most frequently called telephone numbers in a special book that you never take out of your car.
- Use travel time to unwind. Bring along a book on tape or music you really enjoy and make your travel time a positive break. You'll feel more energized and happy when you get to work or home if you enjoyed the ride.

13

Quick Tips for Weddings

For most of us, a wedding is the biggest, most expensive party we will ever throw. With so many components that must come together and so many possibilities for something to go wrong, it's no wonder some brides (and their mothers) don't get much sleep during the weeks leading up to their wedding day. I can't promise you that nothing will go wrong with your wedding; in fact, most people I know had at least one slipup, and they truly do laugh about it now. But don't let planning for your wedding become such a chore that it devours all your energy and eats up your budget and then some. These tips are designed to help you plan for the biggest day in your life.

Quick Tips on Saving Time and Money

- Consider having your wedding at a not-so-prime time; you'll find it cheaper and easier to rent reception space and to find a photographer and caterer.
- Choose flowers that will be in season on your wedding day, or ask your florist to do so. You'll probably save money, and you can be

sure that what you had selected will be available. Some brides choose less expensive silk flowers for the bridesmaids, and their bouquet becomes a gift afterward.

- Consider hiring a bridal consultant. These professionals know from experience where to find the best deals and are able to save you time and money. Get recommendations and create a budget.

- Get everything in writing when meeting with wedding vendors and professionals. This way, everyone knows what was promised and you'll avoid any future misunderstandings. Include all the details in your contract.

- Ask recently married friends for recommendations concerning the caterers, florists, photographers, and musicians you might need for your wedding. You'll save a lot of time finding qualified people if you ask those who have recently used the professional's service.

- Do as much shopping by phone and mail order as you can to save time. Among the things you can order by mail are invitations (several companies advertise in bridal magazines and will send you samples) and gifts for the members of your wedding party.

- Put your bridesmaids to work. Ask them to help you address wedding invitations, pick up out-of-town guests, and run errands as the date of the wedding gets close and your time is limited. After all, bridesmaids are your best friends, and they want to help your wedding go smoothly.

- Computerize your guest list and make duplicate copies. These are real timesavers, since friends and family giving showers or other parties will need them. Print out the list and then check the people you'd like to be included at a particular party.

- Begin writing thank-you notes immediately after your wedding. Also, make sure all of the thank-you notes for your shower are sent promptly and completed before the wedding. One bride I know preaddressed her wedding thank-you notes and then filed them alphabetically. This made writing her thank-yous a breeze.

Quick Tips for Understanding Your Contracts

Before signing a contract for anything—renting a hall, hiring musicians or caterers, engaging a bridal consultant—look carefully at what you are signing. Be sure you know the answers to these questions:

- Can you get your deposit back?
- How much notice is required if you change your mind and want to cancel the contract?
- Are there any hidden charges or fees?
- What if fewer guests than agreed upon RSVP to the wedding? Is the price quoted per person or a minimum event price?
- When is the complete payment due?
- If the wedding is being held outdoors, what provisions are there for bad weather? Who determines what is bad weather, and when is the decision made?
- What if there is an unforeseen event that causes the wedding to be delayed or rescheduled?
- Is everything the vendor is doing for you out-

lined? Who will actually be at the wedding taking the pictures, overseeing the food, directing the family? Get names and details. Add those to your contract. Do not assume anything!

Quick Tips on Shopping for Wedding Attire

• Investigate renting a wedding dress or tuxedo instead of buying one. Ask about this at local bridal shops and tuxedo rental stores. You'll probably save money. (However, if you're the sentimental type and dream of your future daughter wearing the same dress on her own wedding day, go ahead and buy.)

• Have your bridesmaids rent their dresses from the formal-wear shop, which will save them money and keep them from having to buy a dress they'll probably never wear again. (Every bride promises to pick a dress her bridesmaids can wear again, but it's a rare frock that can switch from bridesmaid's duty to any other role.)

• Why not let your bridesmaids select their own dresses? Give them a color swatch and let them pick a dress in that hue. Each one will end up with the dress that's most attractive on her, and you won't have to worry about pleasing everyone. Or choose a few styles in one color and let each bridesmaid choose the most flattering one.

• Wear comfortable shoes to your wedding. You will be on your feet all day and don't want pinched toes or aching arches. If you buy new shoes, do it early so you can break them in. Wear them around the house where they won't get scuffed up.

- Have a clothing run-through the week before the wedding to make sure everything fits. Encourage all immediate members of your family and bridal party to do this if possible. You'll be surprised at the little things that need to be done.

- Stock up on extras such as stockings, handkerchiefs, or breath mints—things that you might need at the last minute. Be prepared!

A Quick System to Keep Track of Guests

- Use index cards to organize your guest list. Each guest receiving an invitation gets his or her own card (so a couple or a family with young kids gets one card) listing name, address, and phone number.

- File these alphabetically in a small box and update the person's card every time you correspond with him or her. On each card, note when the invitation was sent, when the RSVP was received, and whether he or she is coming to the wedding; when the gift was received, what it was, and when the thank-you was sent.

- By having the cards in loose but alphabetical order, you can pull out those you need—people who attended a shower in your honor, for example—and have a handy list of the addresses for the thank-you cards you'll send. When you're done, refile the cards.

14

Quick Tips for Home Buyers

If you could buy a house and make the process hassle-free, you'd do it, right? And who wouldn't? Buying a home is a crazy mixture of the practical and the emotional. On the practical side, you want to find a home you can afford in a neighborhood you want to live in. On the emotional side, you want to love the place you come home to every evening. Buyers often let their feelings take over, leading to a condition known as buyer's remorse when they realize what they've done. While you are house-hunting, keep your emotions in check and follow these tips to make sure your decision is based on sound, practical reasoning—the only known antidote for buyer's remorse.

Be a Smart Buyer

- If you are buying a home in an area with covenants, be sure to read and understand the covenants before signing the contract for a house. Covenants are essentially special laws governing a neighborhood, and they should not be taken lightly.
- Read and understand every contract you

might be asked to sign, including a contract for representation with an agent and a contract to purchase a home.

- Know who the real estate agent is working for. The situation varies from one state to another, but unless you and the agent have an agreement that she is serving as your buyer's agent, assume she is working for the seller, and everything you say may be reported back to the seller (who could use it to his advantage in negotiations over the house).

- The busiest time for home sales is late spring and early summer, because many buyers want to move their families before the start of the school year. If you can wait until this buying season ends, you might be able to negotiate a better price from a seller who is beginning to wonder if his house will ever sell.

- The longer a house is on the market, the more likely a seller is to accept a lower price. Agents won't always tell you how long a house has been on the market, but you can look for clues. Does the photo in the ad show leafless trees, even though it's now early September? That could mean the house has been on the market for months. You can knock on neighbors' doors and ask them how long the For Sale sign has been posted, too.

- Find out if the house is affected in any way by noises, odors, or special problems that you will inherit. You never know until you ask and you should be aware of exactly what you are getting. Consider visiting the house at different times of the day or week to really get to know it.

Keep Track of Houses You Look At

It doesn't take long before all the houses you have seen begin to blur together. Which one had the nice backyard? Which had that horrid turquoise bathroom? Use at least one of these methods to remember important details about houses you look at. After you leave each house, decide what was its best feature and the feature you liked least of all. Use your house-hunting experience to design the house of your dreams, and then don't compromise on the really important features.

- Bring a Polaroid camera with you so you can take a picture of each house; write your notes and reactions on the photo.
- Carry a notebook and make a page for each house, listing pertinent information, your reactions to the house, perhaps even a rough sketch of the floor plan.
- Ask your agent if you can keep the computer printouts from the multiple listing service for each house you visit.
- Keep the flyers that agents prepare showing a photo of the house and some appealing details. Write your thoughts and notes about each home on the appropriate flyer.
- Ask every question you can think of. Get the facts.
- When you first view a house, ask what is not included in the purchase. Make sure you know if the chandeliers, bookcases, elaborate entertainment systems, or items you love most about the house are included. Often the seller takes the decorative or luxury pieces

with him. If you shop smart, you can sometimes get the seller to include in the contract larger items like washers, dryers, and refrigerators. Check it out early on before you begin negotiating, and don't be afraid to ask about things you want.

Investigate the Neighborhood

- Make a test drive from the area you want to buy a house in to your office during the morning rush hour, and repeat the experiment from your workplace to the neighborhood during the evening rush hour. If the traffic is bad, think seriously about whether you want to deal with it five days a week for years to come.
- Find out about the bus or train lines in your area. The more you know, the better informed you'll be later on.
- If the house you're considering is in a neighborhood with a lot of college students, drive around the area on a Friday or Saturday night to see if noisy parties are a problem.
- For a condo or townhouse, drive around the complex in the evening when most of the residents are home, to see if there is adequate parking.
- Meet the neighbors. Talk to them about the pros and cons of the neighborhood.

Keep Your Credit in Check

- Before you even begin looking for a new home, order a copy of your credit report and your spouse's report. You'll find a phone number in the yellow pages under Credit Reporting Agencies. If you don't know which major agencies serve your area, ask at your bank.

- When you receive your credit report, review it very carefully. If there are any items you believe are inaccurate, follow the directions for disputing information. If the negative information is accurate (such as payments past due on an account), you cannot have it removed from the file. Your best bet is to pay off such accounts as quickly as possible, because a mortgage lender will consider the status of all your accounts when deciding whether to grant you a mortgage.
- If you got behind on your bills for a good reason—such as a prolonged illness or job layoff—you can submit a statement explaining the circumstances to be included in the file. Follow the directions supplied by the credit agency to do this.
- Avoid opening new charge accounts or buying big-ticket items like furniture or a car on time payments while you are in the process of applying for a mortgage. Lenders follow very strict rules about how much debt you are allowed to carry at your level of income, and adding the cost of a new bedroom suite to the equation could be enough to disqualify you for a mortgage.

15

Quick Tips for Entertaining

Entertaining can be both exciting and fun as well as exhausting and stressful. Getting everything ready for guests can feel like running an all-day marathon, but there are ways to cut down on the pressure and make entertaining more enjoyable.

The following ideas will help you prepare for the party of your dreams or just for a party of five. Keep in mind that you must allocate the appropriate amount of time to get things ready, especially on the day of your event. However, planning is the key to your entertaining success. Remember, your guests shouldn't be the only ones having a great time!

Quick Tips for Entertaining

- Plan ahead. First choose a date for your party, dinner, or event, and then decide on a theme and guest list. Consider whether you are inviting guests by telephone or sending invitations.
- Get *under*whelmed. Make the party easy. If you really don't have time to be entertaining, hire a caterer. Or if your budget doesn't allow

that, consider purchasing the main course from a caterer or your local grocery store. Our local grocery will poach a salmon or prepare a turkey. Don't overlook the simplest resources.

- Before inviting your guests, consider the chemistry of the group. Add a few new people.
- Choose a theme. Whether you're having a few guests or a few hundred, choose a theme for added fun. You can center your entertaining around a country or a type of cuisine. There are endless options, from a casual backyard barbecue to an Italian feast.
- Consider the likes and dislikes of your guests. Is everyone eating low-fat? Does this crowd prefer fish? Are there any special dietary concerns? Are they chocolate lovers or vegetarians? Aim to please!
- Delegate responsibilities. Whenever possible, assign jobs. Share the event with a friend and host it together, or give your spouse a list of things to do that will help you. Don't be a martyr!
- Stock up days before on basics such as extra bags of ice, coffee filters, paper napkins, dinner mints, trash bags, and containers for leftovers if you think you're going to have a lot of them.
- Clean out your refrigerator ahead of time. The more space you have in the refrigerator for your entertaining, the better off you will be. Every inch will be needed.
- If you are ordering from an outside source, take your own trays to the caterer or the grocery so the professionals can style your food

on them. This way, the food will have your personal touch (and you won't have to return the trays!).

- Prepare what you can the day before. Break the job into manageable tasks and do everything you can in advance.
- Save money by creating centerpieces with things you own instead of flowers. At one party I decorated the table with magnificent dolls that I own, while another time I chose antique toys. Perhaps you have a collection of glass objects or ceramic dogs. Arrange them on the table for a creative setting.
- If you still want to use flowers, consider using single bud vases scattered across your tabletop. Add a burst of color by placing one beautiful spray in each vase for a springtime garden effect.
- If you're more interested in saving time than money, purchase colorful paper or plastic tableware. Use a variety of colors or choose black and add touches of gold or silver. You'll be surprised how fabulous even paper and plastic can look, and your cleanup is only a trash bag or recycling bin away!
- No one will know you are using plastic trays if you cover them with decorative lettuce. The edge of the lettuce can camouflage almost anything and will add an expensive look to your presentation. Remember, presentation is key!
- Add strawberries and mandarin oranges to a mixed green salad for a special look. Little touches like this dress up even the most ordinary greens.
- Have everything cleaned up before your com-

pany arrives. This way you'll have less to do later on, and everything will seem to be under control.

- Make sure your dishwasher is empty before your big event. Dishes will disappear instantly if you're ready for them as soon as they're dirty.

Be a Grocery Store Gourmet—Just Grab It and Go!

To save time and money, you can be a grocery store gourmet! The grocery offers dozens of prepared items that with a personal touch you can transform into gourmet goodies and culinary creations everyone will think you spent hours on. Here are some creative ideas.

- Purchase a bottled Italian salad dressing and add fresh herbs and spices for an added gourmet flavor.
- Purchase fancy colorful toothpicks and miniature hot dogs wrapped in dough. Create a dipping sauce with honey-flavored mustard and you have an instant appetizer.
- Place a layer of smoked salmon or cream cheese on a tortilla and then wrap it up into a tight roll. Slice the tortilla vertically into bite-size pieces and then place them on their side. The spirals of tortilla and filling make fabulous appetizers.
- Purchase a ready-made cheesecake and decorate the top with chocolate shavings. Use a vegetable peeler to create chocolate curls by dragging the peeler along the side of a bar of chocolate. Crush a few chocolate mint

cookies in a plastic resealable bag and sprinkle the cookie crumbs and chocolate curls on top of the cheesecake for a festive touch.

- How about fake filet? Line a tray with fancy lettuce that has a decorative edge. Buy thinly sliced roast beef from the deli department and roll it up tightly to make a wonderful appetizer that looks like filet. Cut the pieces in half to resemble filet and pierce each piece of rolled meat with a colorful festive tooth-pick. Arrange the meat in a wagon-wheel pattern on the lettuce-lined tray. Place a flavored store-bought mustard in the center of the tray and sprinkle parsley around the edge of the bowl. Voilà—instant filet!

- Personalize it! Icing in tubes will allow you to write a message on any store-bought cake, from "Congratulations, Willy" to "Happy Birthday, Justin." You can look like a pro by adding your personal touch.

- Sorbet ices are served at the finest restaurants to clear the palate, and you can use them, too. Use a small melon scooper or ice cream scooper and make sorbet balls from different-colored sorbets. Freeze the balls and then serve them in a fabulous wine or champagne glass.

- Chicken fingers and chicken strips can be bought already prepared, and if you serve them on wooden skewers and add a dipping sauce, you'll look like a gourmet cook!

- Vegetable boats are easy to make. To create one instantly, cut an orange in half and carefully scoop out and remove the orange segments, leaving only the empty peel. Fill the orange cup with precooked spinach soufflé from the frozen food section. This colorful and creative presentation will wow your guests!

Index

Address change, 47
Answering service/
  machine, 9
Appliances, cleaning,
  45

Baby's bag, 24
Babysitters, 26
Bathtub safety, 26
Bill paying, 14
Birthdays, 6
Bulbs, 37
Business cards, 6

Call-back service, 8–9
Cars
  buying, 18
  maintenance, 16
Car-time activities, 25
Change, saving, 16
Check register, 13–14
Children
  chores and, 20,
    26–27
  clean-up tips and,
    21–22

computers and, 26
money-saving tips,
  23–24
routines and, 21–22
safety tips for,
  25–26
snacks for, 27–29
telephones and, 26
traveling with,
  24–25
Chores, 4
  children and, 20,
    26–27
Christmas, 54
Cleaning tips, 42–43
Clean-up tips,
    children and,
    21–22
Clothing, 6
  dry cleaning, 19
  hand-me-downs, 23
  laundry tips, 43–44
  resale shops, 16
  shopping for, 14, 17
  travel, 31
  wedding, 69–70

Computers
  children and, 26
  training, 63
Coupons, 17
Covenants, 71
Credit card charges, 14
Credit reports, 74–75

Daily schedule,
  planning, 4
Deadlines, 61–62, 64
Decorating tips, 56–60
Dishwashers,
  cleaning, 45
Doorstops, 25–26
Drawer organizers, 64
Dressing up, 23
Dry cleaning, 19,
  43–44
Duplicate items, 5
Dusting, 43

Entertaining tips,
  52–54, 76–81
Errands, consolidating,
  4, 16
Estimates, 18, 46

Filing system, 6, 64
Food coupons, 17
Food preparation, 5,
  27, 38–39
Foreign currency, 33
Freezing food, 5, 39–40
Furniture, shopping
  for, 17, 57, 60

Gadgets, timesaving, 6
Garage sales, 46
Gardening tips, 35–37
Gifts, 19, 54–55
Grocery shopping, 4,
  15, 40–41
Guidebooks, 30

Halloween, 53
Hand-me-downs, 23
Hanukkah, 54
Holiday tips, 51–55
Home buyers, tips for,
  71–75
Household cleaning
  tips, 42–43

Independence Day,
  52–53
Interior decorators,
  58–59

Kids on Board
  (Spizman), 25
Kitchen tips, 38–41

Laundry tips, 27,
  43–45
Leftovers, 38, 40
Lists
  grocery, 4, 40
  wish, 18, 24
Luggage, 31

Magazine
  subscriptions, 17

Meal preparation, 5, 27, 38–39

Meetings, 61–63

Money-saving tips, 13–19
  on children, 23–24

Monthly payments, 15–16

Moving tips, 46–50

Mulch, 36

New Year's Eve, 52

Nighttime routine, 21–22

Ovens, cleaning, 45

Overseas travel, 32–33

Packing tips
  moving, 48–49
  travel, 31–32

Painting, 56–57

Parties, 52–54, 76–81

Passports, 32

Perennials, 35

Portable phones, 8

Postage supplies, 6

Priorities, 61–62

Public transportation, 65

Punctuality, 7

Recipes, 38

Refrigerators, cleaning, 45

Resale shops, 16

Responsibility, delegating, 4

Robinson, Sue, 24

Routines, children and, 21–22

Safety tips
  for children, 25–26
  for travel, 33–34

Sales, 15, 51–52

Saving money, 12–19

Secondhand stores, 17, 53

Sewing supplies, 5, 6

Shopping
  for bank, 16
  in bulk, 4, 5
  car, 18
  furniture, 17, 57, 60
  grocery, 4, 15, 40–41

Smart Shopper's Guide to the Best Buys for Kids, The (Robinson), 24

Snacks, for children, 27–29

Spices, 39

Stains, 44

Store brands, 15, 41

Taping television shows, 5

Tax returns, 13

Telephone numbers, 4–5, 63

Telephones
  children and, 26
  timesaving tips,
    8–11, 61
Thanksgiving, 53–54
Thank-you notes, 68
Timesaving tips, 3–7
  telephone, 8–11
Toys, 20, 21, 23–24
Trading phone calls, 9
Travel
  with children, 24–25
  flying tips, 33
  overseas, 32–33

packing tips, 31–32
planning, 30–31
safety, 33–34
to work, 65

Unsolicited telephone
  calls, 10

Wallpaper, 57
Watering plants, 36
Weddings, 66–70
Window cleaner, 42
Wish lists, 18, 24
Work/office, 61–65